Once Upon A Disenchantment

Farhana Kabir

BookLeaf Publishing

India | USA | UK

Presentation by *BookLeaf Publishing*

Web: www.bookleafpub.com

E-mail: info@bookleafpub.com

ISBN : 9789358318869

First edition 2022

DEDICATION

I would like to dedicate this to many people in my life.

To my mum, dad and the rest of my family, a big thank you to you all. You all have always been there for me; whenever I have needed anything, you have always been there for me. Thank you for all your support; your love has always been unconditional and I will always cherish that.

To my dearest best friends Hanan, Kyla, Joanna, Sophie, Bethany and Hayley, a big thank you to you for being there for me always. You always believed in me and you all have always put up with me no matter what. I appreciate the time you all have always had for me. You guys have always been there for me and I adore all of your support. Thank you for everything!

PREFACE

My early childhood memories include falling in love with Disney movies and loving the fairy tale stories that would be read to me by my mother. The traditional tales had quite the impact on me as I was growing up. They enthralled me, taking me into many different worlds. I adored them and this love has carried on even into my adulthood. These early childhood exposures to fairy tales have fostered my love of reading, a love that led me to the path I took in my education and in life. I studied Literature during my university years due to my love of reading.

Since they were such a part of my formative years, these traditional tales are still dear to my heart. However, as an adult, I have gained a different perspective and skills to analyse these tales. No longer can I read them through rose-tinted glasses. Through this analytical exploration, I have realised that there are sides to the tales that are not shown explicitly. I've found that certain morals that these tales show are not as clear cut as they are painted to be. With this mindset, when I read these traditional tales, I found myself wanting to change the narrative, reimagine it. It was this want that created this collection of fairy tale inspired poems.

I wanted to explore the different sides that are not usually explored in these traditional tales and that lead to these different poems. Each poem is inspired by either a specific fairy tale or is an amalgamation of many. As well as writing poems that tackle specific tales; I have also written poems with original narrative inspired by other fairy-tale aspects. I hope that you all enjoy these poems as you join me on this journey.

Fairy-tale

Midnight reigned high at the dark spell
Clock stroke 12 as time fell
The mirror fell, fell hard,
Shattered pieces of his heart.
Scattered, spattered, white glass
Shattered through his force at hand
A thousand memoirs of the lost love,
Raindrops fell, the sky mourned
As Selene lightened the darkness
Moonlight crept, crawling in
Lighting up the shards
Lighting up the blue dark orbs

Closed in agony, regret spread
His house of cards. Crumbling. Dead.

Below, close to drawbridge,
The villagers came. The crowd gathered
Pitchforks, Torches, Flames scattered,
Glowing fireflies, blazing bright
The balcony witnessing the vengeful storm,
As the figure curled in himself.
No more. No light.
The beast bellowed in the night,
Crimson, bloody, ruby, red rose
Petals peeling, crumbling down
Empty, just like his heart, exposed.

Single petal remained, hung in time
Abandoned, discarded, cursed with solitude
Flames engulfed the burning castle,
Weathered by decrepitude

As the memory of those hazel eyes
Remained evermore.

Crimson

Tick Tick Tick
The unseeing beat,
Beat, beat, beat
Continuous and incessant
The noise uprose, incandescent.

Tick Tock Tick,
The hand stroke 12,
Midnight's crimson beast,
Blood-red eyes, burned each time
Honed in on the red hood.

Tick Tick Tock,
The claws held a
hand full of golden lock,
Crimson tears stained the grasses
On the witching hour,
As Selene wept in the
Never-ending Night.

Slumber

Something there is, in the night
That frets and crawls in the dark,
When she lies; and sleeps in bliss,
It sucks her dreams leaving sand in its wake.

Something there is, in the night
It howls in pain and spreads the fright,
In the dark of the night,
The blissful dream rears its head
And turns into a vengeful vision of dread,
She cannot leave; she cannot fight
The unbreakable hold,
The spindle's grip was too strong to fold.
The light goes out at the end of the tunnel;
Leaving fitful dreams in eternal slumber.

Little Red

Hanging on the edge of innocence, she stood
Eyes bright and blue, brimming with curiosity
anew,
Little red cloak, shimmering crimson, she stood,
The path through the woods on her right near her
foot.

Don't go off the path.

Curiosity, curiosity, curiosity hummed abuzz
She walked the path; the path worn and white,
Worn and white, clean and straight, her feet
followed.

Don't go off the path.

She knew it all. She knew it all. But yet;
The twisted dark irresistible road tempted her,
Called to her again and again, enthralling her,
Temptations for the unknown rising high.

It was then her eyes met his;
He was standing in the clearing, a wolf in sight,
With beady blue eyes, wine-stained beard,
A smile painted upon his lips.
What big ears, what big teeth.

She froze at the sight, eyes glazed, and
spellbound
It enraptured her then.

Don't go off the path.

She followed the wolf into the woods,
Off the paths, away from home,
Tangled into the dark thorny woods.
Surrounded by darkness, an eternal night
No light touched her since then.
As if she was falling through a never-ending
rabbit hole,
Off went the years, stripped away.
Years in the darkness, the red cloak dulled,
The reflection in the mirror, a stranger she no
longer knew.

Who are you?

Cinder

Encased in ash and cinders, she was bright
Her gilded, illuminous hair glowed in the light,
Her angel painted luminous smile
Eyes full of beams of dream and light
The sky-kissed eyes, so full of hope and want,
Dimmed as the winters went.

Gilded hair, before oh so golden and aureate
Now as dull as lead
Her dress in tatters, torn and shred,
Eyes now a hollow steel
With trembling hands, smothered in cinder
She remained in solitude,
The light of her smile snuffed out,
Stuck in a never-ending night.

Snow

Shrouded in hazy mist and fog,
Surrounded by snow and frost,
Eyes full of light,
Stood the girl of snow.

Blood-crimson lips and an angel painted blazing
smile
Hair shimmering black as an eternal starry night,
Fair as the winter-kissed dove,
She gleamed like a radiant, untouched rose.

Blood crimson lips and a hollow smile
Her ebony eyes full of tears,
Fair as untrodden snow,
Her hands trembled as scarlet blood
Dripped down, marring the stark white pure
snow.

Blood crimson lips broke down,
The eternal night lingering
Her iridescent ebony hair losing its shine,
The untouched rose
No more, no light.

Tick-Tock

She doesn't know; she doesn't know
The question wandering in the night
The ticking in her mind grows
As the evening draws to a close.

Tick-tock. Tick-tock.
The never-ending clock
Ticking away, the pendulum sways
She strolls through the dark rabbit hole.

A world of wonder, initially thought
But wonder turns to hell
In a frightening turn,
Her scream echoes, broken cries.

Bleeding through, tearing through
Crimson tears alight,
Whispers chipping in her walls
Seeking the light, crawling through the dark.

Clawing out the memory box
Of what wasn't meant to be.
Sweet nothing, sweet void, dark sweet lies
Drags her into the night.

Tick-tock, tick-tock

The ticking ignites,
She stays in the dark
Eyes void of light.

Her crimson lips, a vengeful grin
Light up the sky
Pounding, pounding, footsteps echoes
The ticking ignites.

Tick-tock. Tick-tock
The never-ending clock.
She doesn't know; she doesn't know.
That when it stops:
Silence will fall. Forever More.

Dawn

Born of rose and gold,
She was a beauty to behold
Wrapped in love, adorned in affection,
She was the apple of her father's eye
Holding all of his attention,
He showered her with eternal endearment.

Sun-kissed luminous hair,
Blue diamond eyes and skin so very fair,
She had an angel-painted benevolent smile,
That made anyone sigh.
But all at once darkness struck, fully hostile
The mansion full of hope, love and care,
Fell into despair.

Born of ash and cinder,
Withering, she was stuck in an eternal winter
Trapped in hell, locked away
She was the lost girl in rags,
Cinder stripped her light,
Leaving her in excruciating decrepit decay,
She was stuck in a never-ending night.

Born of despair and cinder,
She was a weary sight to behold
Kept away, left alone

Isolated, she was forsaken.
The darkness was overwhelming,
An abyss that kept getting
Darker and darker.
One hope remained;
Darkness always reigned
Before the dawn.
Trapped in the pits of despair,
She waited for that speck of light
One glimmer of the dawn,
To break through her darkest
Never-ending night.

Briar Rose

It was a grandeur sight to hold
The resplendent soaring tower; enthralling and old
Full of mystery, full of mystique.
Shrouded in fog and mist
It captivated all those around it,
Drawing in hoards of princes and kings.

Surrounded by throngs of imposing, towering trees
It sat in the heart of the forest with ease.
Nestled in the heart of thorns and lingering darkness,
Wrapped in irresistible temptation
Laid the alluring prize,
The sweet holy grail that all wanted to possess.

Glistening gilded sun-kissed golden hair
Crimson red lips and skin snow-kissed fair,
Angel-painted lips curved with eyes shut
And blood red rose laid between her hands,
She painted the picture of a bewitching siren.

Princes and kings, lords and warriors
The list never stopped; all rushed to possess,
Yet the floors were crimson stained,

Tower full of terror and voices strained,
No one could reach the prize.

The Red Door

Twinkling eyes, charming smile, and bright blue
beard,
The master of the mansion was very well
known, yet feared.
With a charming, grand manor and endless gold,
Everything was in his hold.
Yet despite it all, all feared the man in blue.
Year by year he married beauties,
Yet year after year, disappearances occurred
Where did they go? No one knew,
Yet the irresistible gold and life of comfort had
enough pull
That more and more maidens joined hands with
the man in blue.

With glimmering crimson hair and cerulean
eyes,
The new maiden arrived.
Enthralled by the grand space and luxury,
She fell into the enchantment and became the
mistress.
Adorned in gold, she lived in ecstasy,
Mistress of all rooms in the spacious mansion,
Yet despite everything, her attention was caught
by the red door.
The red door which was in the corner of the hall,

A red door full of scratches.

Her curious gaze had been noticed by the master,
His glimmering eyes narrowing just then
With an iniquitous smile,
He placed the bright white key into her hand
And whispered;
Don't open that door.

He left every day, for reasons she did not know;
Alone she wandered in the grand glow,
Yet all the splendour, and luxury was not enough
To curb her cursed curiosity,
For every day her eyes looked at the red door
with ferocity.

Don't open that door.

She knew she couldn't; her promise rang in her
mind,
Spellbound and bewitched,
She longed to know what was behind,
She couldn't stop herself,
She couldn't stop herself.

Don't open that door.

Yet curiosity was burning brightly

For she found herself in front of the door at
night,
Don't open that door.

Key in, turned and turned,
The door swung open
And the sight which beheld her left her burned.

Her eyes met a gruesome blight,
A room fully crimson; everything stained in
blood
Crimson red blood in every sight,
Limbs and torn bodies in every corner,
Silver chains nailed to the wall
Her shaking hands dropped the key.

Frightened and fearful,
She locked the room and washed the key
Yet the stain of her disobedience did not wash
away;
The red stain refused to leave the sight.

When midnight hour struck, he came back,
His twinkling eyes rooted completely at her,
Her shaking hands dropped the damning key
And his eyes gleamed with glee when he noted
the screaming red stain.

Hands caged in by his iron clad-hand,

He dragged her hard, her hands in searing pain
Her heart pounded the closer they got
The second she spotted the closed red door
Her heart raced louder as fear rose.

With crimson eyes she let out a scream
Her hands clutched the key tightly, and she
swung;
The key dug into him hard, his eyes scarlet red
The blue beard, stained scarlet crimson,
Only one survived, the crimson girl standing
still.

The Woods

The woods were not a place to be,
Warnings given out again and again
Mother made it crystal clear,
Do not stray into the woods.

And the girl in red knew such warnings very
well;
Yet she could not help but stray
When she saw the untrodden path.

She walked, she strayed,
She smiled and hopped her way,
Unaware of golden, ominous eyes staring her
way
She hopped and walked her way.

The girl in red cloak standing out in the darkness
When suddenly her path was blocked by a wolf
in sight;
Tall, dark with sharp teeth and a wicked smile
with glee.

Red stopped and stared, not startled just still,
The wolf slithered, salivating at the sight
It reached out and slashed her red cloak.
The wolf expected to see fear flash,

Yet Red simply smiled.
The wolf watched, baffled
His eyes wide, he witnessed a sight
Of Red shifting and distorting
Snarls and growls echoed through the forest.

The wolf's body lay on the forest floor
Red stood tall, her tattered cloak was dilapidated
Yet still in one piece
Her hands and lips; crimson red

She wiped her blood-stained lips
And gave a crimson smile,
The woods were not a place to be.

Sleeping Beauty

She was a delicate beauty,
A fragile, elegant and dainty siren
With gleaming golden hair
And crimson red lips
She was the picture of temptation,
An irresistible sight for
Anyone with eyes.

She was a delicate beauty,
With tempting ruby lips
That beckoned everyone to
Conquer this porcelain doll.
Even the passing Prince couldn't resist
The irresistible temptation of
The sleeping siren.

She was a delicate beauty,
Her eyes, as blue as a stormy ocean,
Opened wide.
Finding herself in an unfamiliar land,
She was overcome with confusion.
Her eyes met the Prince;
The one who won the irresistible prize
That all had longed to take.
He took her and took her hand,
Offering her the land,

She smiled and held his hand,
He did not see her eyes.

Her eyes full of sorrow
Completely hollow, she stood
A doll to be admired.

Winter's Rose

The name rang loud, sweet delight
Leaving an empty sigh,
Now all that's left is a wilted rose
And tears in stinging eyes.

She knew at once, all that's been lost
When longing blossomed into pain,
Eyes watched in fear. The heart grew frosts
No former love remained.

The crimson blush
That shines bright. Fading fast in sight.
Ruby beacon, petals gleaming dark
Bleeding in the night. Fading fast, fading dark.

Winter's touch reaching out,
The ruby light turns blight
Red rose, lost rose,
That shine gone. Waning black sight.
Frozen Swan Song falling,
In everlasting night.

Dreaming

Hazy and misty, everything shone in a rose hue
She was caged in a dreaming state.
A sightseer drifting into the waking world, not
fully awake.
All of her hopes, wants and dreams,
Were completely torn asunder.
The ever-prevailing pull of sleep held in wonder
The pull of the dreaming state was Herculean,
No kiss, no true love
Had the power to break the curse of this
slumber.
Kissed by Nyx, she was pulled under
Caught in the never-ending night,
In the starry eternal night, there was no delight.

Her hopes had been woven like sunbeams
Hopes for a happily ever after,
Yet darkness annihilated them,
No more hoping for a happily ever after.
Hope was like withered autumn leaves,
They slipped through her hands and fell fast.
The waking world was shaking, but
She could not go back
No kiss, no true love
Could possibly break
The immortal hold of Hypnos,

She would not wake.

25

Falling Star

A falling star,
That fell from his heart
It shot through the night,
The shooting star, it flew through the dark abyss
And landed inside her heart.
The lustrous light, shone burning brightly
And its blazing gleam left her blind.

His falling star,
Left her captivated and enthralled,
No moons, no sun
Could leave her so spellbound.
She felt it in her lips, in her hands,
In the tips of her eyelids.
Her heart pounded hard; eyes wide
Blazing gleam left her utterly blind,
All she saw was darkness,
Alone in the dark, she longed for the star she had
gained;
Yet in the dark, she was alone.

The Red Rose

The beautiful rose glowed in the dark night
An illuminous ruby, shining bright.
Through storm, through rain and through snow
Through it all, it stayed in the flow.

A beauty, so untouched and innocent,
It enthralled all eyes, completely magnificent
Captivating and bewitching,
Irresistible, the hands reached out and pulled.

But the rose does not last forever, once pulled
The glowing red dimmed to a dull black,
Devoid of colour, battered by the storm
Discarded, thrown away
The beauty that it once had in its allure,
Now forever devoured,
No longer pure.

Fire

Forged in furious fire, cinders and blood,
She rose amidst the blazing calamitous blaze
Eyes hardened, weary yet not broken
Hands worn from sweeping endless floors,
Bent and buckled, but she did not break.

Forged in furious fire, cinders and blood
She stumbled and fell
Knees scrapped, hands full of blisters
Adorned in tattered rags,
Glass slipper shattered like her dreams
Yet that did not stop her steps;
She crawled the rest of the path.

The path was thorny and untrodden
But that did not hinder her,
Forged in furious fire, cinders and blood
She never gave up.

Frozen

Shrouded in ice and encased in the cold
The lone rebellious rose laid alight,
Amidst the barren land
Defying all odds, defying the possibility
The rose thrived atop the frozen ground.

Beautiful sight it was; glowing and gleaming
bright
A shining sight that attracted all sight,
But all that gleamed would dull
No one noted the man with an iniquitous smile,
Whose eyes were full of malice.

Eyes observing the shining, magical rose,
Calamitous hands clutched the miraculous rose
and pulled.
Scarlet red blood pooled into the frozen ground,
Staining the ground in an overflowing cascade
The red turned to black, petals crumbling,
crushed.

Shrouded in ice and encased in the cold,
Was a brilliant red rose
Now all that remained was a blood-stained
ground
And lingering darkness.

Looking Glass

The looking glass was gleaming
Shining clear, smooth and beautiful
It was the picture of perfection.
One look and you could see everything,
See even sides of you that you've never seen
before
She looked into the looking glass then;
Who was the fairest of them all?

Fair skin, ruby lips and emerald eyes,
Eyes shining with delight,
A smile appeared in the mirror
A smile like her,
But a smile not her.
Youthful adolescence,
Naïve innocence,
Desired by all in sight.

The reflection was perfect, so perfect;
The youth being true perfection.
Her own youth disappeared with age,
She was not wanted on stage,
They all craved the beauty of the youth,
Eyes desiring the little girl in snow,
Perfect lips, perfect smile, perfect skin, perfect
eyes

And a youthful smile,
She lost it all now with time.

Replaced by the girl who was
Who was blooming just then,
She numbly wondered;
Would even the girl in snow
Reach this stage of life
Where all beauty is snuffed out
By Chronos's vicious power.

Alice

Something is. Something is
In this mind
of Dark and Light,

A hollow pain. Empty. Devoid.
A casket of tears, not enough to fill
A hollow pain, lost of light
No way out, lost, lost, lost still.

Hollow, hollow, hollow
The dark abyss of night,
Hollow, hollow, hollow
The shattered looking glass in sight.

Looking glass, broken glass
Crimson stained shard,
A cry in the night,
Morpheus silenced and marred.

Cold, wispy hands
Dark. Dark. Dark.
Cold wispy hands
Of Phobetor, grasping strong
A laugh in the night, the echoing swan song

The rabbit hole, never-ending,

No light, Phobetor taken all,
Sweet, Sweet Alice,
Wake no more
Sweet, Sweet Alice,

Dream forevermore.

Beauty to Behold

She was adorned in gold
A beauty to behold,
Gilded hair that shone with light
Yet caged in the ominous
Dingy tower, she was caged untold.

She was adorned in gold
A beauty to behold,
Shining bright gold luminous eyes
But her smile was hollow,
Full of loneliness and sorrow.
Isolated, no friends in sight,
Trapped in the tower,
She craved for the light.

She was adorned in gold
A beauty to behold,
But her face was hollow
Her heart lost in the unbearable pain;
A casket not enough to fill her tears,

She was adorned in gold
A beauty to behold,
Enough to attract his gaze
Dark eyes that observed from afar,
Eyes which craved the beguiling beauty.

Lonely she was, just a meeting was enough
Enchanted she became,
With the man who snuck in,
Innocence lost; she fell into the abyss.

She was adorned in blue
A beauty to behold,
With empty eyes, empty smile
Beside the prince, she was his doll
To adorn the royal palace.

Surrounded by many, she stood above
Yet it did not fill the emptiness in her heart.
Incarcerated inside the golden palace;
A beautiful caged bird,
She stood alone, feeling empty,
Forever cocooned in a chrysalis of solitude.